For

Copyright © 1970, 1992
Peter Pauper Press, Inc.
202 Mamaroneck Avenue
White Plains, NY 10601
All rights reserved
ISBN 0-88088-737-0
Printed in China
16 15 14 13 12 11

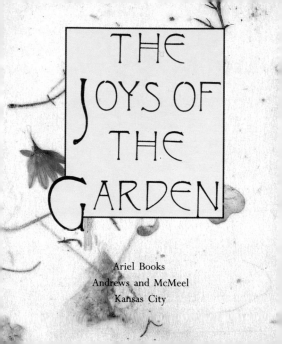

THE JOYS OF THE GARDEN

Ariel Books

Andrews and McMeel

Kansas City

10 9 8 7 6

ISBN: 0-8362-3010-8

Library of Congress Catalog Card Number:
91-77099

Design: Diane Stevenson/SNAP•HAUS GRAPHICS

*S*ome of the best lessons
are learned from mistakes
and failures.

Ask always, "Is there a better way?"

*B*uild on faith rather
than on doubts.

Move forward in the
hope of what can be accom-
plished, and do not be held
back by what cannot be done.

See the possibilities in the new and do not be paralyzed by the difficulties to be overcome.

*D*iscover a sense of mission that life may be important and purposeful for you rather than dull and purposeless.

$\mathcal{M}$ easure values in
terms of service to others
rather than benefit to self.

The love of money is the root of all evil, but the possession of it is an opportunity for much good.

There is no limit to the good a person can do, if he does not care who gets the credit.

$\mathcal{A}$n uncommitted person is a person without direction in life. He is like a ship without a rudder, and plenty of power but no direction.

*L*ife is still rich in things
to which one can give
oneself—social causes to
serve, truth to be discovered,
beauty to be created, friend-
ship to claim one's loyalty. All
of the great secrets of the
world have not yet been
discovered.

The strongest things in the world often seem the weakest. For instance: gentleness is stronger than cruelty, patience is stronger than impatience, mercy is stronger than revenge, and love is stronger than hate.

To whom much is given,
much is expected.

*S*uccess should be
measured not so much by
the position one has reached
in life as by the obstacles
which one has overcome
while trying to succeed.

*H*appiness consists not in having many things, but in needing few.

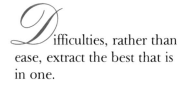

Difficulties, rather than
ease, extract the best that is
in one.

There is no limitation to forgiveness; no injury so gross that it ought not be forgiven.

Ecidujerp spelled back-
wards is prejudice; either way
it does not make sense.

Wherever there is forward movement, there is bound to be turbulence.

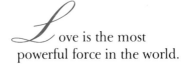

$\mathcal{L}$ ove is the most powerful force in the world.

*I*t is noteworthy that the so-called seven deadly sins—pride, covetousness, lust, envy, anger, gluttony, and sloth—are all matters of attitude, inner spirit, and motives.

The potter pulls the clay for the handle of a pitcher from every possible side. With people, as with clay, outside pressure, properly absorbed, creates inner strength.

*N*ever accept the negative until you have thoroughly explored the positive.

A person needs to be loved the most when he deserves to be loved the least.

Genius is infinite
patience.

To be one of thousands
who have worked together to
make possible some worthy
event in history—that is our
opportunity.

*I*f you constantly compare yourself with others, you may become either unhappy or boastfully proud, for there will always be people greater or lesser than you. Remember that your mediocre gifts may contribute more toward the success of

some project than the
extraordinary talents of
another. Believe in the
worthiness of what you can
do and be content in doing
the best you can.

$\mathcal{A}$round every person is a sphere of influence beyond which he cannot pass; but within range of that circle he is powerful and free.

That which you are able to do may seem small compared with what others accomplish, or compared with what you would like to do—but your little, if done well, may count for more than some more ambitious task, poorly done.

*Y*ou can spend so much time fretting about the past and things that cannot be changed, and worrying about the future and things which may never happen, that you lose the joy and fullness of the now, the present.

*P*robably the greatest need of the world today is for reconciliation. In order to establish a good relationship with others one must first admit his full share of responsibility; and if one has been wronged then he must be willing to forgive unconditionally—for partial forgiveness is not forgiveness at all.

*M*isfortune may cause a setback, but it need not mean defeat. It is not what happens to a person, but how he reacts that is important. What seems a handicap may prove to be an asset or an opportunity.

*I*f boiling water is poured into an empty glass it will crack, and if ice-cold water is poured into it, it will also crack; but if hot and cold water are mixed together before pouring, the glass will not crack.

*I*t is one thing to have more to do than you can get done in one day, but it is quite a different thing, and inexcusable, to neglect doing those things you could or should do each day.

A person who does not understand another's silences will not understand his words either.

Promotion is two-thirds
motion.

What you do, what you
say, what you are, may help
others in ways you never
know. Your influence, like
your shadow, extends where
you may never be.

Undertakings entered into half-heartedly often lack the extra or the plus that can lift them over the hurdle. Enthusiasm may mark the difference between success and failure.

*T*ruth is never wrong, but the purpose or motive for telling the truth needs to be considered. Is the purpose of telling the truth to hurt or to help another? It makes a difference how the truth is told, for words, even though truthful, can bring such offense that the damage done may offset the intended good. Therefore one should "speak the truth in love."

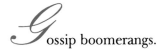Gossip boomerangs.

Absolutes change.

*P*erseverance makes
many things possible.

The secret of happiness is to learn to live within one's limitations, whether they are physical, financial or circumstantial.

Whether you have little ability or great ability and excel in many things, whether you have one talent or ten talents, is not of the greatest importance. What you do with what you have is what counts!

*T*he success of a team
depends upon how well the
members play together and
this means being willing to
lose one's identity for the
sake of the team.

There are divisions in our community relationships which disturb and separate us, but the things which unite are actually greater than the things which divide us.

One has no right to say
of any good work that it is
too hard to do; or of any
misfortune that it is too hard
to bear; or of any sinful habit
that it is too hard to
overcome. To do so is to
admit defeat, and to lose by
default. Help is always
available.

You can never tell when
you do an act
Just what the result will be;
For with every deed you are
sowing a seed,
Though its harvest you may
not see.
AUTHOR UNKNOWN

*T*oday's burden can be endured. It is when tomorrow's burdens are added to the burdens of today that the weight is more than one can bear.

*T*hank God every morning
when you get up that you
have something to do which
must be done, whether you
like it or not. Being forced to
work, and forced to do your
best, will breed in you
temperance, self-control,
diligence, strength of will,
content, and a hundred other
virtues which the ungrateful
will never know.
CHARLES KINGSLEY

*I*n the soul of human
beings at their best there is
an unconquerable spirit.

*T*reat people as if they
were what they ought to be
and you help them to
become what they are capable
of being.

GOETHE

For every evil under
   the sun
There is a remedy, or there
   is none;
If there is, seek and find it,
But if not, then never mind it.
AUTHOR UNKNOWN

*P*eople grow apart needlessly. Most troubles could be avoided if people would give a little, be a little less self-centered, and try a little more to help each other.

He is wise who gives
what he cannot keep in order
to gain what he cannot lose.

$\mathcal{H}$old your temper and keep your patience under all circumstances, for when you yield to vengeance you destroy or retard reconciliation.

$\mathcal{E}$verything you do is of
importance because much
which needs to be done will
be done only if you do it.

We never know how heavy
a burden another person
may be carrying.

*N*othing can stop the
person with the right attitude
from pursuing his goal.

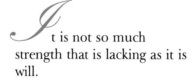

It is not so much
strength that is lacking as it is
will.

Our satisfactions in life
will be in proportion to our
contributions.

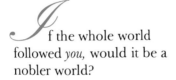

*I*f the whole world
followed *you*, would it be a
nobler world?

There is nothing noble in being superior to some one else; true nobility lies in being superior to your previous self.

$\mathcal{T}$he limits of faith are the
mental barriers or doubts of
one's own making.

When it is dark enough,
you can see the stars.
CHARLES A. BEARD